To: Megan
Happy Reading

From:
Grand aunty [illegible]

July 2023

PARENTING WITH PURPOSE

A Guide to Raising Children with Resilience, Emotional Intelligence, and Empathy

By Gillian Quahe
Illustrated by Rae Yap

Cover and Illustrations by Rae Yap

Dedication

First and foremost, to God who makes everything possible and beautiful.

To my wonderful husband, Derrick. Who supports and makes sacrifices for me and the family so that I can pursue my passion.

To my beautiful daughter, B. You are my driving force and inspiration to be the best I can be for you and for Daddy.

To my fur baby, J. Your company at night when everyone else is sleeping means the world to me.

To my parents, Yenna, Erwin, and also my twin mama, Yenni. Who have loved, encouraged me, supported my dreams, and never told me I could not do it.

I love you all fiercely and deeply always.

To my wonderful support system, Emmelyn, Daniel, Ian, Sam.
My pillars of strength and sanity, Joyce, Bri, Nupur, Kelly, Anoosha.

Without the guidance of Alycia, Trinity, Nancy, Krystal, this book would not have existed.

Last but not least, Clarissa, the one who started me on this journey of pageantry, rediscovery & self-love.

Forward

Welcome,

My name is Andrew and I have been given the honour and pleasure of writing the foreword to Gillian's new book.

I believe this book is important because early child development sets the foundation for lifelong learning, behaviour and well-being. The experiences children have in early childhood shapes the brain and the child's ability to learn, socialise with others, and respond to daily stresses and challenges with resilience.

I met Gillian in 2013 at a school in Singapore. Gillian's background and experience was a wealth of knowledge to the school. She was our 'go-to' when anyone needed advice or mentorship, which she delivered both wisely and empathetically in a down-to-earth and light-hearted manner. Her approach was exactly what was needed, and it helped our staff through many challenging situations.

Gillian's qualifications and broad teaching experience gives credibility to her book. This can be seen by the advice and anecdotes given in these pages. I have been involved and worked in the entire education system and its always a treasure to meet someone who "knows their stuff."

It was a privilege to read and revisit Gillian's advice. She shares her guidance in clear, easy-to-understand bite-size sections that deliver proven and effective strategies for behaviour management in children.

Yours sincerely,

Andrew Schamschurin
PhD, MSc, BSc (Hons), Grad.Dip.Ed

Letter From the Author

My dearest friend,

You hold in your hands my life's work thus far - my passion, my pride, and joy. It's a compilation of advice, insights, and thought-processing break-downs of my journey as an educational therapist and a mother.

Writing a book was always a bucket list item for me. I knew I wanted to write an illustrated children's book, but I never thought that my experience and knowledge as both an educational therapist and a mum could ever collide into forming a singular entity which I could use in my tool kit to guide me on my journey of being a parent.

Being an educational therapist with over 12 years of experience and having seen over 150 neurotypical and neurodiverse clients in Singapore, Melbourne and London, becoming a mum was singularly the most daunting thing to me. Having crossed paths with so many parents who struggle with their own insecurities of raising a socially confident and emotionally intelligent child, I became acutely aware of my own shortcomings.

I realised there are no manuals that provides guidance or validation to the way one parents. We'd hit a wall, become absolutely overwhelmed with responsibilities and we go down a spiral. In these times, a simple 'you're doing well' from someone, was incredibly reassuring to my completely frazzled self. When one gets stuck , they'd have to search for strategies to cope and manage a situation, and no one was around to point out potential triggers so they could learn to mindfully manage. As a result, I decided to write a book that collated my knowledge. A visually rich and intuitively accessible book which guides and supports parents through their journey, gently posing questions that encourages a shift in perspectives, and bring attention to little details they otherwise would not have considered.

In true ET fashion, where one thing can always be looked at, used, and interpreted in different ways, this book can also be enjoyed in multiple ways:

1. With your child, the illustrations were specifically created to encourage conversations about emotions,
2. As a coffee table book - a great conversation starter for those with, without or thinking of having children people,
3. In the loo, when your having your alone time and need some reading materials because you've left your phone outside.

I truly hope that you and your loved ones enjoy this book as much as I have enjoyed creating it, and I pray that it will bring many light-bulb moments, great memories and wonderful parental milestones, and that through it your relationships with become fuller, stronger, and more meaningful.

Tag me on @soulpurposeintl to share your stories and journey with a willing and non-judgemental partner, I would love to continue to be a part of your journey, because afterall, we're all in this together!

With much much much love,
Gillian

PARENTING WITH PURPOSE

A Guide to Raising Children with Resilience, Emotional Intelligence, and Empathy

By Gillian Quahe
Illustrated by Rae Yap

Table of Contents

BOUNDARIES AND COMMUNICATION

TANTRUMS

TECHNIQUES FOR RAISING CHILDREN WITH LOVE

PROMOTING CHILDREN'S SELF-GROWTH

Chapter One

BOUNDARIES AND COMMUNICATION

Safety:
Boundaries help keep children safe from harm. By establishing rules about what is and isn't acceptable behaviour, parents can protect their children from danger.

Consistency:
Boundaries create consistency in a child's environment, allowing them to feel secure and confident. When children know what to expect, they are less likely to act out or become anxious.

Development:
Children learn from their environment, and boundaries can help promote healthy development. By setting limits and guiding them towards positive behaviours, parents can help their children develop important skills and values, such as self-control and empathy.

Respect:
Setting boundaries teaches children to respect themselves and others. By establishing rules about behaviour and communication, parents can teach their children how to treat others with kindness and respect.

Communication:
Effective communication builds strong relationships with children. By talking openly and honestly with their children, parents can create a safe space for their children to express themselves and share their thoughts and feelings.

DON'T FORCE A CHILD TO SAY 'SORRY'

Explain the emotions behind it.

A forced apology is insincere and doesn't help your child learn. Instead, tell your child that you understand their feelings and talk them through the emotions they felt and ask why they acted or reacted the way they did.

This teaches them how to identify their feelings and demonstrates empathy.

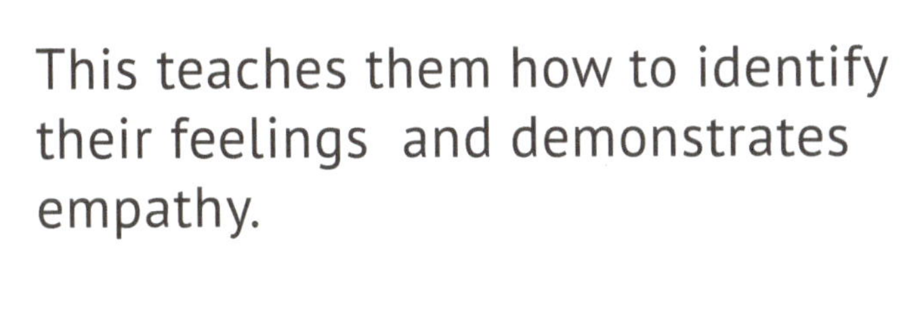

SHOUTING OR YELLING BREEDS DISTRUST AND FEAR

If someone yells at you, it doesn't make you feel good, does it?

How would you feel about that person after that incident? What are the chances of you wanting to interact with this person again?

As adults, we can make the decision to set boundaries after the incident, but children can't.

MAINTAIN CONSISTENCY

If you say one thing and do another, your child would get confused and can't begin to build trust.

If you say, *'Five more minutes and then we'll go brush our teeth,'* make sure to come to get them in five minutes to brush their teeth.

Parents often wonder why their child doesn't listen to them, but it's because the child has realised that when the caregiver says *'five minutes,'* they often come back 10-20 minutes later, or the time can be extended indefinitely.

This sends the message that they don't actually have to stop what they are doing in five minutes.

FOLLOW THROUGH WITH WHAT YOU SAY

If you tell your child that they can't have ice cream at grandma's house because it triggers their asthma, stick to it. Or if you say that you won't buy any more toys at the mall because you just bought some last week, stick to it.

If you don't follow through, your child will learn that you don't mean what you say and may start pushing boundaries.

This can lead to them using your inconsistencies against you when they get older and wiser.

For example, they may say, "*Why can't I have it? You said no last time, but you still let me have it.*"

DON'T TAKE THINGS PERSONALLY

It's important to look at your child's behaviour or reaction objectively.

For example, if your child hits you in the face, it's essential to consider if it was an accident or if they're trying to communicate something to you. If you're missing their cues and react by yelling, it wouldn't be fair to them.

Imagine how you would feel if someone scolded you for something you tried to communicate that you didn't want to do.

It's essential to maintain a calm and rational mindset when dealing with your child's actions and reactions to ensure that you're responding appropriately to their needs.

TELL THEM WHAT TO EXPECT NEXT TO ENSURE SMOOTH TRANSITIONS

For example, you could say, "*We're going to put on our PJ's, and then we'll brush our teeth.*" When children know what comes next, it can reduce their anxiety about what will happen.

Even as adults, we generally prefer knowing what's going to happen next to prepare ourselves mentally, physically, or emotionally.

Predictability can help reduce anxiety and create a sense of stability for your child. By providing a clear roadmap of what's to come, you can make transitions smoother and less stressful for both you and your child.

DON'T SPEAK ILL OF YOUR CHILD IN FRONT OF THEM

It's crucial to be mindful of our words when discussing our children in their presence, even on difficult days. Instead of focusing on the negative aspects, emphasize the positive moments.

For instance, if someone asks about their day and it was challenging, reframe it by saying, "*We had some tough moments, but my child showed bravery and resilience in difficult situations*."

As a therapist, when parents inquired about the session in the presence of the child, I would always highlight the positive aspects and commend their achievements. It's essential to address issues in a positive manner, fostering encouragement and confidence in the child.

Often, children lose that motivation to try or are scared to try because they don't feel safe to try. It's like 'What's the point of trying if my parent is just going to negative things about it or not recognise my efforts in trying'.

LET YOUR CHILD SPEAK FOR THEMSELVES

This builds independence, confidence, and develops a child's social and interpersonal skills.

If they are feeling shy or are not ready to make that connection, acknowledge their feelings and say, *"Not right now? That's ok, we can try again later."* By saying this, we are not shaming them for the way they feel but recognising they need some extra time to feel up to the task.

Just as with adults, sometimes we don't feel like saying hi to someone. Sometimes we need an extra push, or a little tiny pep talk to muster some courage to start or initiate a conversation.

GIVE A SPECIFIC TIME FRAME AND STICK TO IT, AS MUCH AS POSSIBLE

Imagine you're in a restaurant and you placed your order for food. Some time goes by and your food hasn't arrived, so you ask the waitress to check on the food. They come back and say soon.

Some more time goes by, the food still hasn't arrived, so you call the waitress over again and ask about your food. The waitress replies again, it will come soon. Some more time goes by, and the food still has not arrived!

How would you be feeling at this point? Irritated? Annoyed? Not to mention HANGRY. When the waitress comes back and says, Ma'am/Sir, it'll be another 5 minutes, would you trust what she says?

When are we going to Disneyland? **9am.**
What time are we going to leave Gran's house? **5pm.**

Avoid giving vague timelines. When are we leaving the party? Soon. There's no sense of time and children can't gauge. If they repeatedly ask that question, how will they know exactly when the next thing is going to happen?

Chapter Two

TANTRUMS

Tantrums are something that every parent has difficulty dealing with. It is the irrationality of all and the why won't you or why can't you just listen to me?

I think the most helpful strategy I have used, is to first calm myself down. I take a deep breath and close my eyes for a few seconds. I allow space for myself to feel these feelings and space for my child or client.

I begin to process what needs are not being met for them. Are they hungry, tired, overstimulated, or frustrated at a task? Once I figure that out, provide care and a possible solution, the tantrum dissipates quickly.

REGULATE YOUR EMOTIONS

We hear this a lot, but what does it mean exactly?

It means having the ability to exert control over what you are feeling in the moment. Can you stop yourself from yelling or punching a pillow if you feel frustrated? If you feel sad, can you stop eating an entire tub of ice cream? If you feel happy, you stop yourself from doing a goofy happy dance because you're in the middle of an important Zoom call?

As a caregiver, we will experience the need to regulate our emotions ALL THE TIME. Children will push our buttons and constantly test boundaries. We must remember that it isn't the child's responsibility to avoid doing these things. In fact, testing boundaries is part of a toddler's job description. It's important to figure out what to do to calm yourself down when you start to see red.

This can be taking three deep breaths, counting to ten, or stepping away from the situation for the time being. When you're calm, I promise the situation is less likely to escalate further, and the meltdown will be resolved sooner.

TANTRUMS ARE NOT MISBEHAVIOURS

They are an overwhelming expression of emotions. Toddlers experience everything for the first time, and they have yet to learn how to regulate and deal with their emotions.

Their acting out is how they express themselves.

Imagine that you've lost your voice and someone takes away your phone while you were trying to send a super important work email. What would you do?

Would you bang the table or clap your hands to get their attention?

How would you feel emotionally?

Angry, annoyed that someone took your phone while you needed to do something, and frustrated because they didn't pay attention to you while you were trying to communicate.

That would be the adult version of a tantrum.

DON'T PARENT WHEN THE CHILD IS IN THE RED ZONE

Wait till they are in the green zone before attempting to, if not, they are not able to process anything.

Imagine you wake up, you discover your water heater is broken, you ran out of coffee, you forgot your phone and some stranger shoved you out of way so they could get on the train, as a result you missed your train.

So you had to have a cold shower, haven't had your caffeine, and don't have your phone so you couldn't inform work you are going to be late.

Imagine the level of frustration and anger you would be experiencing. You finally get to work, and your manager tells you that the work you produced was not up to standard *(needed some tweaking)* and based on how you were carrying yourself this morning, an attitude adjustment.

How would you feel? Would you hear anything the manager has said? Would you be open to hearing anything they said?

EMBRACE THE MESS

Having a child is messy, but through the mess is also how a child learns.

When they drop a toy, they learn about gravity and cause and effect.

When they throw food, they learn about texture and how it interacts with their environment.

As adults, we can potentially adjust the space to reduce mess, but it's important to let children explore and learn through their natural curiosity.

So, don't worry too much about the mess, and enjoy the learning opportunities that come with it.

PUT YOURSELF IN THEIR SHOES

Try to see the world through your child's eyes when tantrums occur.

Toddlers may seem to tantrum over the littlest things, but they have yet to learn and understand that most situations are not permanent.

They have yet to learn how to manage big emotions and cannot regulate or control themselves.

Even as adults, we sometimes have difficulty doing this despite having years of experience and exposure to all kinds of emotions.

How can we expect a child to do this without providing them with the proper strategies to cope?

PRACTICE SELF-AWARENESS

Recognise your feelings and reactions. Think about why you react or feel that way. Is it a trigger? Did something happen to make you feel this way?

Take a moment to pause and think about the feelings you are experiencing before reacting and responding to a situation that has triggered you.

Practicing self-awareness can help you regulate your emotions and respond in a way that is productive and positive for both you and your child.

Chapter Three

TECHNIQUES FOR RAISING CHILDREN WITH LOVE

This is always the intention, to raise children with love. We do the things we do, out of love. Sometimes though, it does not always translate that way, especially to a child who is not mature enough to rationalize adult behaviours, speech, and mannerisms. As adults, we often forget that although children can understand a lot, they have yet to learn how to manage their actions, thoughts, and emotions. It is only through being shown and explained repetitively, that they will not only learn but remember.

DISTRACTION DISMISSES EMOTIONS

Distraction dismisses emotions and fails to acknowledge a child's feelings at the moment.

It is the opposite of connection and does not address the underlying emotions. Over time, the child may learn to suppress or ignore their feelings, leading to emotional difficulties later in life.

As adults, we may also resort to distracting ourselves from uncomfortable emotions.

However, using distraction as a coping mechanism should be followed up with a discussion about emotions.

For example, "I noticed you were upset when mommy left. I know its hard to be away from her. We'll see her after we have a play and a nap."

GO WITH THE FLOW

Be flexible. It's not always about what you want, how you want to play, or what you want to do.

Consider the goal of the activity.

Sometimes a child wants to draw circles only, use one colour when colouring, or play with one toy the entire day.

At some stage, they will get to the other things.

Allow them the freedom.

REACTING TO RUDE OR LOADED COMMENTS FROM CHILDREN

We may wonder how we can stop them from saying it again or explain to them that it's an inappropriate thing to say without actually telling them what it means.

The question we need to ask ourselves is whether they actually know what they're saying or if they're simply repeating something they've heard.

For example, if a 5-year-old says "*pick up the soap*," his mother may be mortified and sternly tell him not to say that.

However, what does a child typically do when told not to do something?

They do it again.

As an observer, it's clear that the child is trying to get attention, and bad publicity is still publicity. So the next time a situation like this arises, it's essential to have a quick mental check to see if the child understands what they're saying.

If not, it's best to ignore it, and they will likely stop saying it. Alternatively, you could say, "*I'm not sure what to say to that. Let me think about it, and I'll tell you what I think in awhile.*"

It's crucial to follow through on this statement and not leave the child hanging, as children don't forget easily.

In summary, it's important to understand whether your child knows the meaning behind what they're saying before reacting. If they don't, ignoring it may be the best option. Additionally, it's okay to take a moment to gather your thoughts and respond thoughtfully to the situation.

RAISING EMOTIONALLY INTELLIGENT CHILDREN

One way to do this is by talking through our emotions and how something made us feel. After a situation occurs, take time to reflect on your feelings and actions.

Consider whether your reaction was appropriate or inappropriate, and what you could do differently in the future.

By openly discussing our emotions, we teach our children that it's okay to feel and express their own emotions as well.

We also demonstrate that it's possible to regulate our emotions and respond in a thoughtful and constructive way.

This can help children develop important skills like empathy, self-awareness, and problem-solving, which will serve the well in all areas of life.

DON'T DISMISS A CHILD'S FEELINGS

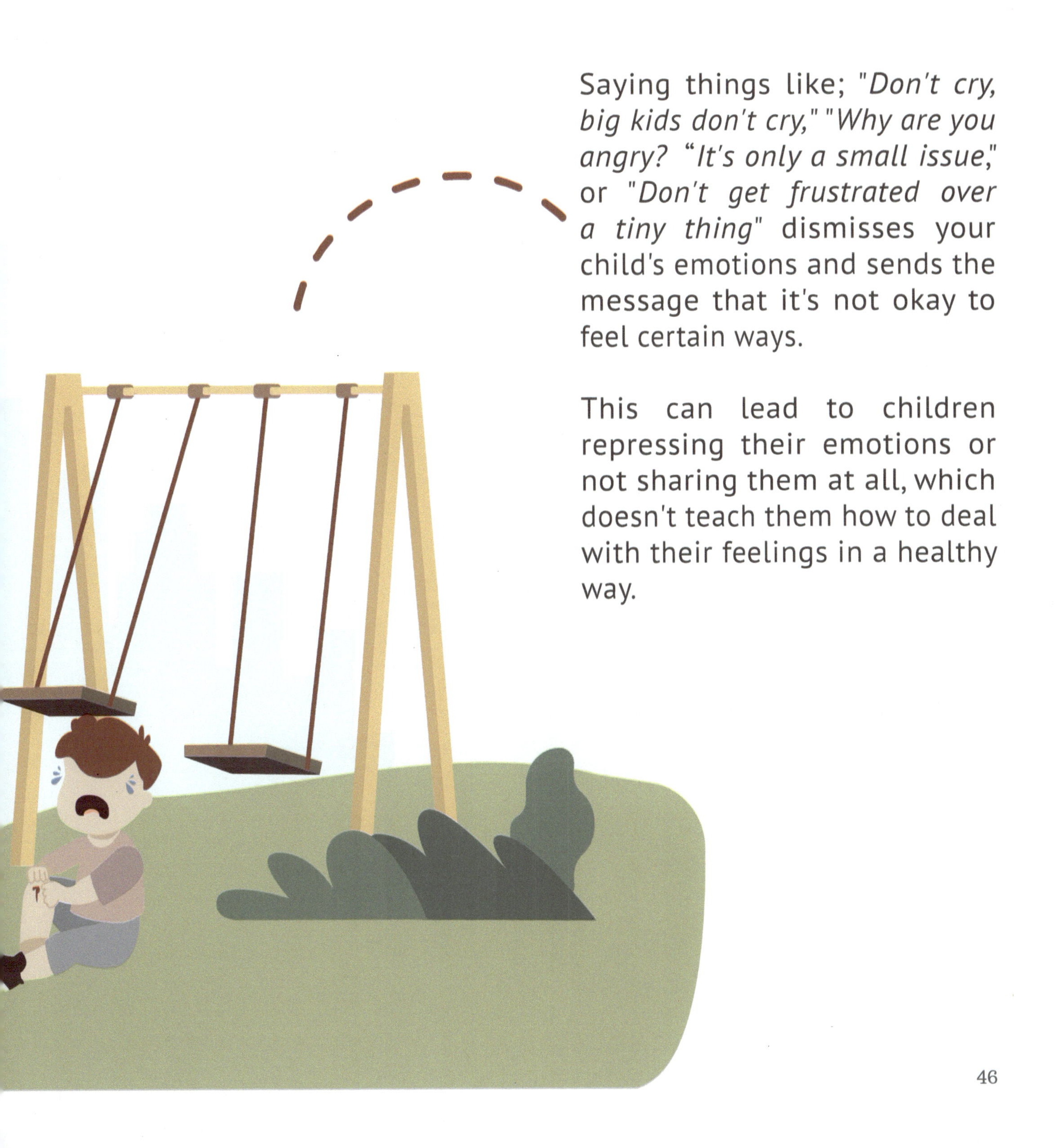

Saying things like; "*Don't cry, big kids don't cry,*" "*Why are you angry?* "*It's only a small issue,*" or "*Don't get frustrated over a tiny thing*" dismisses your child's emotions and sends the message that it's not okay to feel certain ways.

This can lead to children repressing their emotions or not sharing them at all, which doesn't teach them how to deal with their feelings in a healthy way.

APOLOGISE TO YOUR CHILD

Model the behaviour you want to see. You want your child to learn from their mistakes and apologise when they've done something wrong, rather than force them to. We need to show them how it's done.

As parents we are humans too, even though our children look to us as magical and all powerful beings, capable of anything and everything, we have our slip-ups and when we do, we need to show them we can reflect on our behaviour and say sorry.

WHAT YOU LABEL YOUR CHILD IS WHAT THEY WILL BECOME

I hear these labels frequently, 'naughty', 'rude', 'fat' or' lazy'.

Parents, grandparents or aunties and uncles will often say to a child, *"you're so naughty",* when they don't finish their food, or throw their food or when they do something funny or throw a tantrum.

This can become a self-fulfilling prophecy.

Children don't want to be that but they get told that, so they must be that. It is important to remember, positive labels can be just as impactful as negative ones.

It is crucial to use labels that reflect a child's true potential and avoid using labels that can limit their growth and development.

BE KIND BUT FIRM

Lay down expectations and boundaries clearly to avoid confusion and reduce surprises. Think like Mary Poppins, "I am kind but extremely firm.' Sometimes there is some confusion with setting boundaries and being rigid, or being gentle and being a pushover.

It can sound like this:

I can see you still want to play AND its time for dinner.

You recognise their needs but are also telling them what is expected of them.

You don't want to brush your teeth AND we will do it together. Let's see who can get their toothpaste on faster?

Make it game. Kids love whimsy and fun, who doesn't? When you can make mundane things fun, it really makes it more bearable. Imagine if you had to do the same things over and over again, like a job of sending out those credit card bills statement, print, staple, fold, put in the envelope, seal it, repeat till infinity. After a while, if you tried to make a game out of it, would it help make time go a little faster, make it more enjoyable?

I see that you are not ready to clean up AND what did we agree on?

Prior to them playing, make a deal with them that they need to clean up when it's time to. If they renege, gently remind them that they made a deal. It also teaches them to honour their words and follow through with that they said.

WAIT AND OBSERVE BEFORE REACTING

Children experience many things at once and need time and repetition to process and make sense of these experiences.

As adults, we have had more time, experience, and repetition, making it easier to process and react quickly.

For children, it's like a trial-and-error situation. We encourage them to explore and learn by giving them space to try.

So before reacting, wait and observe to understand what your child is experiencing and how they respond. This can help you respond in a more helpful and supportive way.

Chapter Four

Promoting Children's Self-Growth

Builds Confidence:
When children are supported in exploring their interests, taking on challenges, and achieving small successes, it boosts their self-esteem and helps them develop a positive self-image.

Develops Independence:
By encouraging them to take on age-appropriate responsibilities, make decisions, solve problems, and learn from their experiences, children gain a sense of autonomy and become more self-reliant.

Cultivating Resilience:
Self-growth involves facing challenges, setbacks, and failures. Resilience is a valuable life skill that enables children to cope with difficulties and adapt to change throughout their lives.

Enhances Overall Well-Being:
When children are given opportunities to grow, learn, and develop their skills, they experience a sense of fulfilment and satisfaction. This can lead to improved emotional well-being, reduced stress levels, and a more positive outlook on life.

LET YOUR CHILD EXPERIENCE BOREDOM

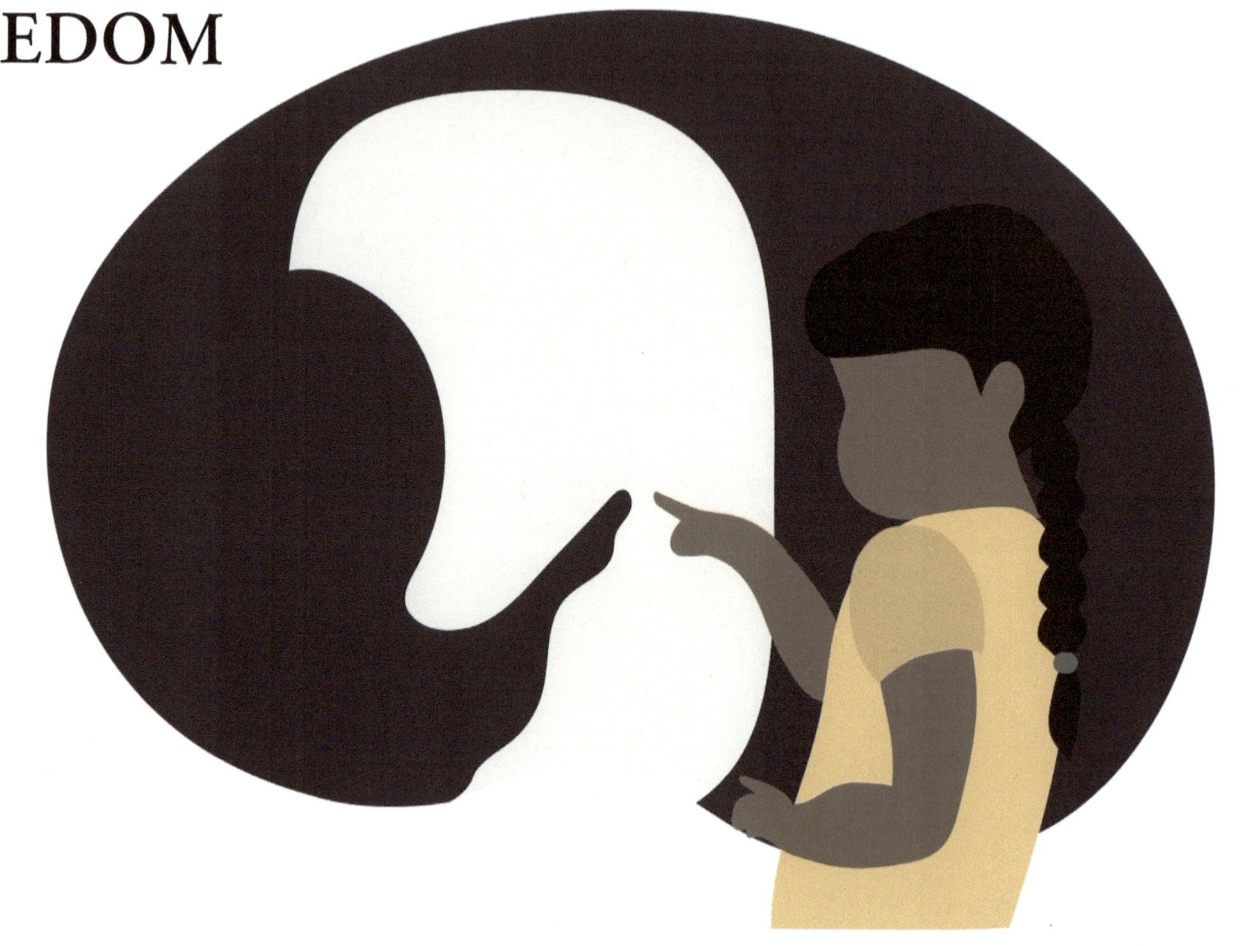

Children need time and space to explore independently, without the direction of an adult. It's often the adult who feels uncomfortable with boredom and feels the need to constantly entertain or view boredom as a waste of time.

We may then try to occupy our children's time with academic or extracurricular activities, and get upset when they can't sit still or be quiet.

But how can we expect our children to do something we don't nurture, encourage, or model ourselves?

BABIES ARE DEPENDENT, NOT HELPLESS

Babies are actually quite capable.

They communicate their needs through cues, although we often miss them. By observing and recognizing patterns, we can pick up on these cues. Infants can tell us when they're tired, hungry, need a break, overstimulated, or not feeling well.

For example, moving their fists to their mouths indicates hunger, avoiding eye contact suggests tiredness or over-stimulation, and turning away from stimulation means they need a break.

Being aware of these cues can reduce frustration for both caregivers and babies.

LITTLE WINS HELP YOUR CHILD SUCCEED

Don't completely finish a task for them when they can do it themselves or are trying to learn how to.

For example, when twisting a bottle cap, twist it just enough to make it easier to open, and then give it back to them to fully twist it open.

When they realise that they can do it, they gain confidence and it also builds independence.

INTERACT WITH PEOPLE FROM DIFFERENT BACKGROUNDS AND CULTURES

Interacting with a diverse community of people can help your child develop empathy, respect, and tolerance for others with different beliefs, customs, and traditions.

Through these experiences, children can learn to celebrate differences and embrace diversity, making them more well-rounded and compassionate individuals.

DON'T UNDER-ESTIMATE HOW MUCH YOUR CHILD KNOWS AND UNDERSTANDS

This is especially important at the time when the child has yet to learn how to speak verbally. This also goes for children who are non-verbal.

Continue to speak to them and explain things at an appropriate level for them, even though they might not be able to verbalise their understanding just yet.

CHILDREN ARE BORN NOT KNOWING WHAT FEAR IS. FEAR IS LEARNT.

Fear can be a healthy and adaptive response to danger, but excessive or irrational fear can interfere with a child's development.

For example, some people may have had traumatic experiences with dogs in the past, and if they haven't addressed or managed their fears, they might react in a seemingly exaggerated way when encountering a dog while caring for a child.

They might tell the child that the dog is scary and could bite, or they might jump anxiously to the side when accidentally getting too close to a dog. When a child witnesses this kind of behaviour, they learn to fear dogs as well, regardless of the dog's breed, temperament, or size.

Parents and caregivers can help manage these fears by providing safe and supportive environments, model coping strategies, and gradually expose them to the feared stimuli in a supportive and controlled manner.

About the Author

Gillian is an educational therapist and parent education advocate. She studied in Melbourne, Australia and obtained both her undergrad in Early Childhood Education and her Masters in Education (Specific Learning Difficulties) at The University of Melbourne. She has taught in Melbourne, London and Singapore over the last 12 years.

She is a mum to a gorgeous little girl and a smaller than usual french bulldog. She currently lives in Singapore with her husband, Derrick and their family.

Her other passions include crafting, calligraphy and also cooking. Gillian would most often be found at home with her family.

About the Illustrator

Rae graduated from Ringling College of Art and Design majoring in Computer Animation. She is a versatile graphic designer, illustrator, and motion designer with nearly a decade of experience in agency and freelance settings. She is all about creating designs that captivate, communicate, and evoke emotions. With a diverse background spanning various industries, Rae brings a fresh perspective to every project. A trend enthusiast, infusing her work with a whimsical touch and staying on top of all the fun design trends. From digital illustrations, animations, media concept to branding, Rae consistently delivers high-quality and exceptional results.

raeraeart.com

Ingram Content Group UK Ltd.
Milton Keynes UK
UKHW050857020723
424394UK00003B/18